INSIDE BATTLE MACHINES
BATTLESHIPS

Iowa-class WWII battleship firing her guns in action

by Chris Oxlade

HUNGRY TOMATO.

USS *Texas*, a huge battleship that fought in both world wars

Contents

[Highlighted words appear in the glossary]

BATTLE MACHINES
BATTLESHIPS

Warships are the weapons of a navy, which is a country's military force at sea. These battle machines protect their own ships and attack enemy ships, aircraft and forces ashore. Since their invention, there have been dozens of different types of warship and many are no longer around. Today the main types are **frigates**, destroyers, cruisers and aircraft carriers – the largest of all modern battleships.

USS *Nimitz* aircraft carrier

Battle of Trafalgar, 1805

Old versus new

The two pictures show how warships have changed over time. Above centre is British Vice Admiral Nelson's flagship **HMS** *Victory*, with other ships of the line at the Battle of Trafalgar (see pp.14–15). These were wooden sailing ships armed with dozens of cannon. On the left is the steel-built supercarrier USS *Nimitz*. Its weapons are its devastating strike aircraft, so this enormous ship presents a whole new world of battleship technology.

THE FIRST
WARSHIPS

Nobody knows who invented the first boat, but it's certain they invented it more than 10,000 years ago. Early boats were simple craft made of logs or bundles of reeds, but slowly boat builders learned to build bigger. They also invented new technologies, such as sails and steering oars. As long as 4,000 years ago, specialized warships were going into battle.

Egyptian warships

There are pictures of sailing boats on the River Nile in Egypt, painted about 5,500 years ago, with **hulls** made from reed bundles. Similar boats, armed with soldiers, could have been the first battleships. The Egyptians soon developed strong, seaworthy **merchant ships**, made of wood. Warships called **galleys** were based on these, but galleys were longer, narrower and faster. They carried archers and spearmen for attacking enemy craft.

Triremes

The most powerful warship of Ancient Greece was the trireme, a galley powered by three banks of oars on each side. These big ships had a strong **keel** along the length of the boat, with frames to support planking for the hull. The trireme became the main Greek fighting ship. Later ships had catapults on board for firing huge darts and stones at the enemy.

Uniremes and biremes

The earliest warships built by the Ancient Greeks were galleys called uniremes ('uni' for one, and 'remus' for oar, which meant the ships had one bank of oars). The main weapon was a ram sticking out from the **bow** (front). It was used to smash enemy ships before soldiers boarded to fight the enemy's crew. Around 750 BCE, the Greeks developed the bireme, with two banks of oars for better speed.

Trireme rowers

A typical trireme had three rows of 25 or more oars on each side, making at least 150 in total. The oarsmen sat on different levels inside the hull, sliding backwards and forwards on leather cushions as they rowed. The crews had to be well-drilled to row fast and manoeuvre their ships accurately in battle. Some navies experimented with massive galleys with a thousand or more rowers!

Greek trireme

Length:	38 metres
Beam:	6 metres
Crew:	200
Oars:	170
Top speed:	13 kilometres per hour

ANCIENT
SEA BATTLES

The great powers of the ancient world, including the Greeks, Romans and Persians, all built large fleets of fighting galleys. When the navies met in battle, hundreds of opposing biremes and triremes would try to ram and sink each other, and there would be fierce hand-to-hand fighting on deck. Among the greatest battles was the Battle of Salamis, in 480 BCE.

The Battle of Salamis

Salamis was a great sea battle between the Greek and Persian navies during the Greco-Persian Wars. The battle took place off the Greek coast, in the channel between the island of Salamis and the port of Piraeus. The Greeks, who had about 370 galleys, lured the bigger Persian force (about 800 galleys) into the narrow strait, and then attacked, sinking 300 Persian ships with the loss of just 40 of their own.

Salamis key facts

When:	480 BCE
Where:	Greece
Number of ships:	800 Persian / 370 Greek
Losses:	300 Persian ships / 40 Greek ships
Victor:	Greece

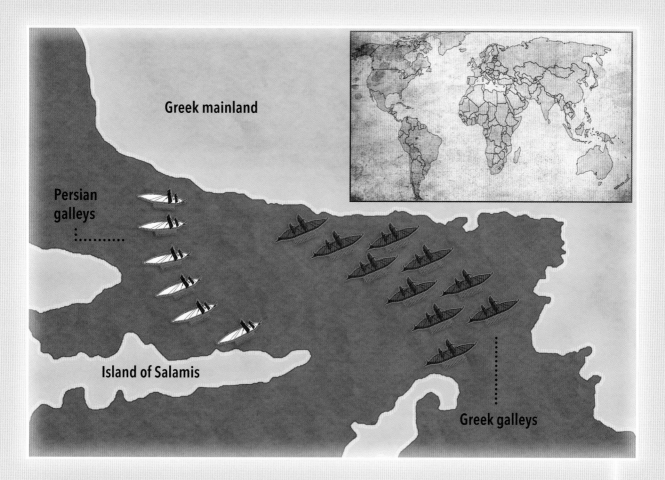

Greek mainland

Persian galleys

Island of Salamis

Greek galleys

Battle tactics

The Greeks won the Battle of Salamis because the Persian ships could not manoeuvre in the narrow waters where the Greeks chose to attack them. Rowing at top speed, the Greeks rammed into the Persian ships, holing them and stopping them from escaping. Greek soldiers swarmed onto the rammed ships and captured or sank them.

Greek fire

A new weapon was introduced in battles between galleys more than 1,000 years after Salamis. It was invented in the 7th century CE, and was called Greek fire. The main ingredient was oil or tar. It was heated, ignited and squirted through a nozzle at enemy ships, setting them ablaze and causing panic.

MEDIEVAL WARSHIPS

Warships changed very little between ancient times and medieval times, 1,000 or so years later. They continued to have a single square sail and lots of oars. But in the 12th and 13th centuries, new ship technologies were invented, such as the **stern rudder**, deep keel, triangular sail and full rigging. These made ships more manoeuvrable and able to sail against the wind. Guns were also invented, and so by the 15th century there were large, strong warships with three masts, armed with rows of deadly cannon.

Mixture of square and triangular sails

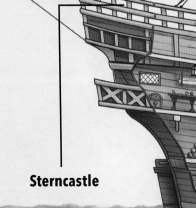

Sterncastle

The Armada

The Spanish Armada was a large fleet sent to invade England in 1588. It included 40 warships and 19,000 soldiers. While the Armada was at anchor, the English sent in ships set on fire, creating chaos. They then attacked with guns that had better range than those of the Spanish, and defeated the Armada. It was one of first sea battles to feature cannon.

Stern rudder

Ship's cannon

The cannon was made possible by the invention of gunpowder. At first warships had only cannon mounted near the bow. Gradually, cannon got larger, and ships got more of them. The cannon were arranged along the sides of a ship, pointing out through gun ports. They fired iron cannonballs as heavy as 27 kilograms, which smashed and splintered the hulls and masts of enemy ships.

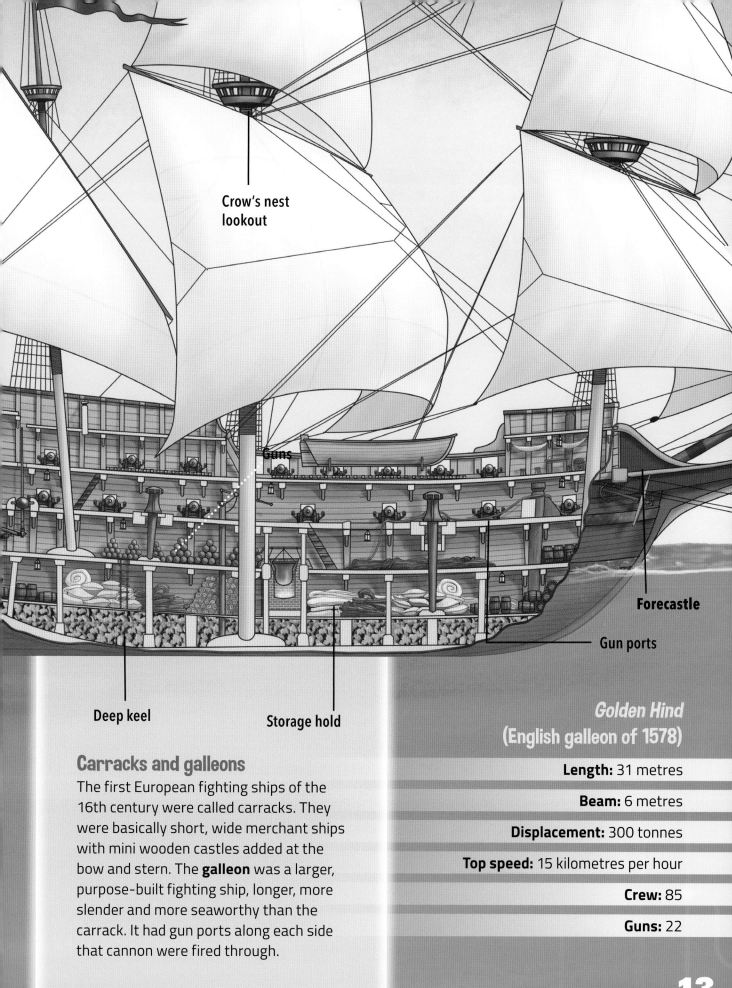

Crow's nest lookout

Guns

Forecastle

Gun ports

Deep keel

Storage hold

Carracks and galleons

The first European fighting ships of the 16th century were called carracks. They were basically short, wide merchant ships with mini wooden castles added at the bow and stern. The **galleon** was a larger, purpose-built fighting ship, longer, more slender and more seaworthy than the carrack. It had gun ports along each side that cannon were fired through.

Golden Hind
(English galleon of 1578)

Length: 31 metres

Beam: 6 metres

Displacement: 300 tonnes

Top speed: 15 kilometres per hour

Crew: 85

Guns: 22

SHIPS
OF THE LINE

The galleons of the 16th century were used for exploration and trading, as well as for fighting. But by the 17th century, warships were specialized ships, built just for fighting. They boasted two or three gun decks and dozens of guns. These ships were known as 'great ships' and later, 'ships of the line', because they fought in line formation, one behind the other.

HMS *Victory*

This is one of the gun decks of HMS *Victory*, the flagship of the British fleet that fought at Trafalgar. *Victory* was a 'first-rate' ship of the line, with 104 guns. The guns rolled back on their carriages when they fired. During a battle, this deck would have been a terrifying place, filled with smoke, noise and shouting as crews reloaded and fired their guns as quickly as possible.

The Battle of Trafalgar

By the start of the 19th century, sailing warships were powerful fighting machines, capable of terrible destruction. Major battles were fought between powerful ships of the line. At the Battle of Trafalgar in 1805, a fleet of 27 British ships defeated 33 French and Spanish ships.

HMS *Prince*

Length of keel: 40 metres

Beam: 13.7 metres

Guns: 100

Crew: 780

HMS *Prince*

Built in 1670, *Prince* was one of the 'great ships' of the English king, Charles II. It carried 100 guns on three gun decks, with the biggest firing 19-kilogram cannonballs. *Prince* was not only deadly, but also beautiful – covered in delicate carvings and gold paint.

Officers quarters

Crew quarters

Masts down to the keel

Rudder

Gun deck

Frame made of oak timbers

IRONCLADS

In the 19th century, the world of warships changed completely. Steam engines replaced sails as the main means of propulsion, and big guns firing shells replaced cannon firing iron balls. Iron became available to shipbuilders, and soon wooden ships were covered in plates of thick iron armour. These were the **ironclads**. The American Civil War (1861–65) saw some of the first battles between these new warships.

Ironclad riverboat

This riverboat was built in 1856 to work as a ferry and river steamer on the Mississippi River in the USA. The US Army bought the boat in 1861, covered it in iron armour, added six guns and renamed it **USS** *Essex*. The ship took part in several fights with **Confederate** ships. It was damaged several times, but never sank.

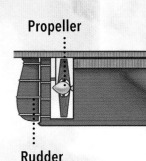

Propeller

Rudder

The Battle of Hampton Roads

One of the first ironclad battles was between USS *Monitor* (right) and **CSS** *Virginia* (above). It took place near Hampton, Virginia, and became known as the Battle of Hampton Roads. *Monitor* and *Virginia* fired at each other, *Monitor* using its armoured rotating turret gun. Both ships were damaged, but not badly, and so the battle ended as a draw.

Confederate ironclad

CSS *Virginia* was a Confederate ship of the American Civil War. It was built from the remains of a badly damaged, wooden steam-powered frigate. Iron armour plates were added above the deck, a ram at the front and guns all round. The *Virginia* was one of the first warships to be fitted with a propeller rather than paddle wheels, which were used on previous steam-powered ships.

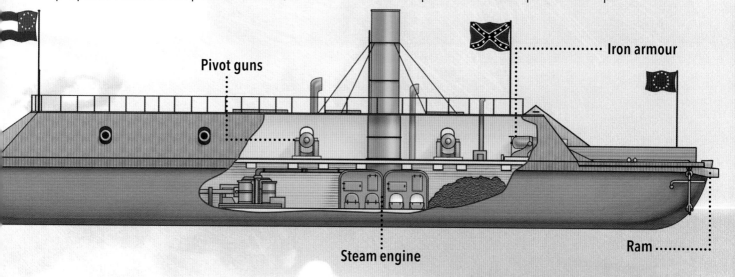

Pivot guns

Iron armour

Steam engine

Ram

Breeches and shells

Ironclads were fitted with a new type of gun. Unlike the cannon on ships of the line, the new guns were breech-loaders: loaded from the back not the front, which was much quicker and easier. They also fired exploding shells instead of solid balls. The shells – pointed cylinders full of explosive – were more accurate and flew further than cannonballs.

CSS *Virginia*	
Length:	84 metres
Beam:	16 metres
Displacement:	4,064 tonnes
Guns:	10
Crew:	320

BATTLESHIPS

By the beginning of the 20th century, warships were not just clad with metal – they were made completely from metal. The biggest warships were covered with thick, hardened steel armour for protection against shells and **torpedoes**. They were armed with big guns that could hit targets more than 10 kilometres away. These powerful ships were the first battleships.

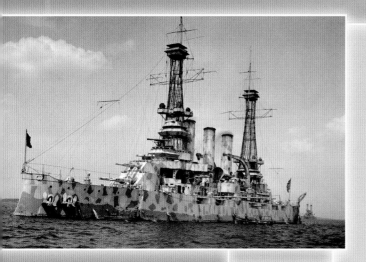

USS *New Jersey*

This US Navy ship was the American version of the battleship, and typical of the battleships that served in World War I. It was armed with four 305-millimetre guns and eight 203-millimetre guns, and operated by 812 officers and men. The sides of the hull were painted in camouflage pattern to make the ship harder for submarines to spot against the background waves.

HMS *Dreadnought*

One of the very first battleships was HMS *Dreadnought* (meaning 'fear nothing'). It was such a groundbreaking ship that battleships built after it were also known as 'dreadnoughts'. HMS *Dreadnought* was launched in 1906. As well as its armour and big guns, it had a new type of engine – the **steam turbine** – to power its four propellers. These created much less vibration than normal steam engines, and allowed a better top speed.

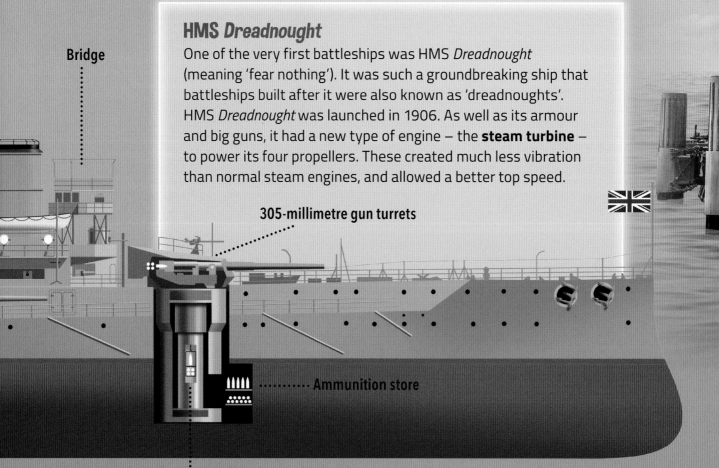

Bridge

305-millimetre gun turrets

Ammunition store

Ammunition elevator

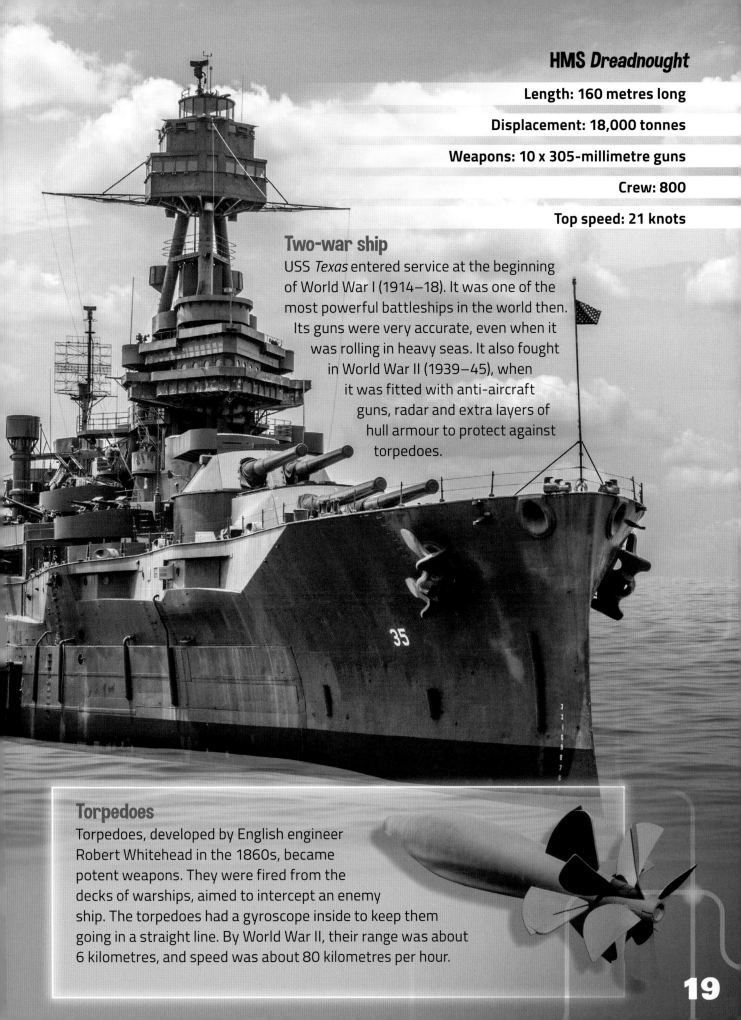

HMS *Dreadnought*

Length: 160 metres long

Displacement: 18,000 tonnes

Weapons: 10 x 305-millimetre guns

Crew: 800

Top speed: 21 knots

Two-war ship

USS *Texas* entered service at the beginning of World War I (1914–18). It was one of the most powerful battleships in the world then. Its guns were very accurate, even when it was rolling in heavy seas. It also fought in World War II (1939–45), when it was fitted with anti-aircraft guns, radar and extra layers of hull armour to protect against torpedoes.

Torpedoes

Torpedoes, developed by English engineer Robert Whitehead in the 1860s, became potent weapons. They were fired from the decks of warships, aimed to intercept an enemy ship. The torpedoes had a gyroscope inside to keep them going in a straight line. By World War II, their range was about 6 kilometres, and speed was about 80 kilometres per hour.

THE RISE OF
CARRIERS

The first experimental aircraft carriers were built around the end of World War I. They were made by adding flat decks on top of other warships or merchant ships. By the start of World War II, carriers were powerful weapons. They were vital for forces fighting thousands of kilometres from home, where there were no runways on land for aircraft to use. Their aircraft attacked enemy ships and targets on shore.

Carriers in the Pacific

American aircraft carriers operated in the Pacific Ocean during World War II, fighting Japanese forces. The USS *Essex* and its sister carriers weighed 27,500 tonnes and carried 100 aircraft. Later in the war even larger ships joined them. Planes from US carriers sank the Japanese battleships *Yamato* and *Musashi*, the two largest battleships ever built.

Battleship barrage

Battleships such as the USS *Idaho* worked alongside aircraft carriers. In the Pacific they fought against Japanese battleships, protecting fleets of ships. They also supported troops invading Pacific islands by attacking defences with their guns from far out at sea.

Runways at sea

The top deck of a carrier is a runway used for take-off and landing. The ship's bridge (the room from which the ship is controlled) and the runway control tower is in the superstructure to the side of the deck. On World War II carriers, aircraft took off under their own power or were launched by a steam catapult. Landing was tricky, especially in rough weather, and required great skill from the pilots.

Hangars

Aircraft were stored on deck, or in hangars under the flight deck, where they could be serviced and repaired. A lift carried the planes between the deck and the hangar. Some ships had armoured decks; others had simple wooden decks that were easier to repair. Carrier aircraft had folding wings to save space on deck and in the hangar.

MODERN
WARSHIPS

Modern navies operate a range of different warship types, each with its own role. There are small, fast attack craft; **mine** hunters; frigates, destroyers and cruisers, which attack other ships and submarines, and defend against aircraft and missiles; giant aircraft carriers; and assault ships for landing troops on beaches. The main weapons are missiles rather than guns.

Stealth ships

Many modern warships feature stealth technology, designed to make them difficult for enemy ships to detect. Like all stealthy warships, this Swedish *Visby*-class corvette has flat surfaces on its hull and superstructure. This makes it hard for enemy radar systems to spot. It also has hidden exhaust outlets for its gas turbines, so that heat-seeking missiles can't find it. It carries remote-control **submersibles**, which search underwater for explosive mines.

Missile defences

The greatest threat to a modern warship is the anti-ship missile, fired from another ship or aircraft. Warships no longer have armour as battleships did. Instead they have anti-missile and anti-aircraft defences that shoot down approaching airborne threats. These defences include a close in weapons system (CIWS), which uses radar to track incoming missiles and aircraft, and a cannon that fires thousands of rounds per minute at the target to bring it down.

On the bridge

A ship's crew control the ships from the bridge, normally high up towards the front of the ship. All the controls are electronic, and the ship is steered with small joysticks instead of traditional wheels. This is the bridge of USS *Zumwalt*, a US Navy destroyer armed with **guided missiles**. Information from radars, cameras and other equipment is displayed on monitors.

MODERN
AIRCRAFT CARRIERS

Aircraft carriers are the biggest ships in modern naval fleets. They are incredibly potent warships not because of on-board weapons, but because of the aircraft they carry to attack targets in the air, at sea and on land. These giant ships are mobile air bases that can take the fight to any part of the world as part of a battle group.

The strike aircraft are stored on deck or in the hangar under the deck. Helicopters and reconnaissance planes are also carried.

The main flight deck has take-off and landing areas.

Anti-aircraft and anti-missile missiles

Deck operations

Flight-deck crews organize aircraft for catapult take-offs, landings, refuelling, re-arming, servicing and repairs. They move aircraft between the flight deck and hangar with four huge electrically powered lifts. Every crew member has a specific job to do and wears colour-coded clothing to show what that job is.

24

Nimitz-class carrier

The biggest aircraft carriers in the US Navy (which are also the biggest aircraft carriers in the world) are the *Nimitz*-class supercarriers, such as the USS *John C. Stennis*, seen here operating in the Pacific Ocean. It is powered by two nuclear reactors, which means it hardly ever has to refuel.

Nimitz-class carrier

Length: 333 metres	
Beam: 77 metres	
Displacement: 105,000 tonnes	
Top speed: 56 kilometres per hour	
Propulsion: two nuclear reactors	
Aircraft: 90 fixed wing aircraft and helicopters	
Crew: 5,000+	
Range: almost unlimited	

Four steam-powered catapults accelerate the aircraft to flying speed.

Command centre or "island" contains the ship's bridge

Steel wires across the deck catch landing aircraft and stop them quickly.

Aircraft elevators move aircraft between the deck and hangar.

Close-in weapons system for missile defence

Power for the engines and other systems comes from two nuclear reactors.

A reconnaissance plane ready to be catapulted into the air

INSIDE A
WARSHIP

This is a modern warship of the British Navy. It's a Type 45 Destroyer – one of the most advanced warships in the world, bristling with high-tech equipment and weapons. It's a guided-missile destroyer, and its job is to protect aircraft carriers and other ships from aircraft and missile attack. Its radar can track 2,000 targets at once, and it carries dozens of missiles to fire at approaching planes and missiles.

Operations room

In the heart of the ship there is an operations room, where the crew keep an eye on enemy aircraft and ship movements. Information from the ship's radars, sonars and other sensors is shown on screen. Missile launches and gunfire are controlled from here, too.

The main gun fires 25 rounds a minute. It has an ammunition store below, in the depths of the ship. There are also other anti-aircraft and machine guns for defending the ship.

Missile silo: **surface-to-air-missiles** are stored here

The missile system tracking radar can detect targets 400 kilometres away.

Type 45 Destroyer

Length: 152 metres

Beam: 21 metres

Displacement: 8,500 tonnes

Missiles: 48 x Aster anti-aircraft and anti-missile

Top speed: 56 kilometres per hour

Range: 13,000 kilometres

Crew: 191

Bridge

The on-board helicopter carries torpedoes and missiles to attack ships and submarines. There's a hangar next to the landing deck.

D32

The ship is powered by gas turbine engines. These operate generators, which produce electricity for the motors that turn the propellers, and for the other systems.

Operations room

TIMELINE

c. 10,000 BCE
By this time people were making journeys in simple boats

750 BCE
The Ancient Greeks develop the bireme, a galley with two sets of oars

1545
Henry VIII's warship the *Mary Rose* sinks during battle

1588
The Spanish Armada, a great fleet of Spanish galleons, is defeated by English ships

1805
British ships, led by HMS *Victory*, defeat a French and Spanish fleet at the Battle of Trafalgar

1916
The British and German fleets meet at the Battle of Jutland, the only major naval battle of World War I

1918
World War I ends

c. 1200
The stern rudder is developed in Europe, having previously been invented in China

7th century CE
Invention of Greek fire, a weapon that sprays burning oil onto enemy ships

480 BCE
The Greek navy defeats the larger Persian navy at The Battle of Salamis

3,500 BCE
Evidence for the first sailing ships comes from this time

1670
HMS *Prince*, the flagship of Charles II of England, is launched

16th century
Galleons – large fighting ships armed with cannon – are developed

14th century
Cannon are used on ships for the first time

1860s
In England, Robert Whitehead develops the torpedo

1862
USS *Monitor* and CSS *Virginia* take shots at each other at the Battle of Hampton Roads, during the American Civil War

1914
The battleship USS *Texas* enters service with the US Navy, as World War I begins in Europe

1906
HMS *Dreadnought*, the first proper battleship, is launched

1939-45
Aircraft carriers and battleships play a major role in World War II

2013
The US Navy's first stealth warship, the USS *Zumwalt* is launched

1972
USS *Nimitz*, the US Navy's first supercarrier, is launched

FACT FILE

- At Trafalgar in 1805, the French and Spanish lost 22 of their 33 ships; the British lost none.

- There is evidence from Ancient Greece of truly giant triremes. One report describes a ship 130 metres long, with hundreds of oars 18 metres long, operated by 4,000 rowers.

- HMS *Victory*, Nelson's flagship at the Battle of Trafalgar, had a top speed of 16 kilometres per hour, which was very fast for a ship of its size.

- USS *Monitor* sank in a storm in 1862. Recently, parts of it have been raised from the seabed, including the rotating gun turret.

- The Spanish Armada was defeated by the weather as much as by English ships. Storms blew the Armada into the North Sea, and more storms destroyed up to half the ships.

- The USS *Zumwalt*, a US Navy stealth ship, has a low radar 'signature', so that it looks like a small fishing boat on a radar screen.

- Around 250 ships, with a total of 100,000 crew on board, took part in the Battle of Jutland in 1916, off the coast of Denmark. A German cruiser sinking is depicted here.

GLOSSARY

Beam
The width of a ship at its widest point

Bow
The front of a ship

Confederate
The name of one of the sides in the American Civil War (the other being the Union)

CSS
Short for Confederate States Ship, a ship fighting for the Confederate forces during the American Civil War

Displacement
A measure of how much a ship weighs

Forecastle
A castle-like structure at the bow of a ship. In medieval times, archers were positioned there to attack, and it was also a defensive stronghold for the crew

Frigate
The smallest but most numerous kind of modern warship

Early naval mine

Galleon
A large cargo and fighting ship of the 15th century, powered by sail

Galley
An ancient type of warship, powered by many oars and a square sail

Guided missile
A missile that is guided to its target by a laser or by detecting heat coming from a target

HMS
Short for Her Majesty's Ship, a ship of the British Royal Navy

Hull
The main body of a ship

Ironclad
A warship with a wooden hull covered with iron plates for armour

Keel
A strong structure along the bottom of a ship, like a spine

Merchant ship
Any non-naval ship

Spanish galleon

Mine
An explosive device placed placed underwater that explodes when a ship hits it

Propulsion
The type of engine that make a ship move, such as a steam turbine, diesel engine or nuclear reactor

Rudder
A flap at the back of a ship used to make the ship turn left or right

Steam Turbine
A fan-like rotor that spins when steam flows through it

Stern
The back of a ship

Sterncastle (or aftercastle)
A castle-like structure at the stern of a ship

Submersible
A small, often remote-controlled vessel that moves underwater

Surface-to-air missile
A guided missile fired from the ground or from a ship aimed at a target in the air, such as a fighter jet

Torpedo
A weapon fired from a ship or submarine that travels through the water to its target

Union
The name of one of the sides in the American Civil War (the other being the Confederacy)

USS
Short for United States Ship, a ship of the US Navy

Torpedo

USS *Cairo*, one of the first American ironclad warships

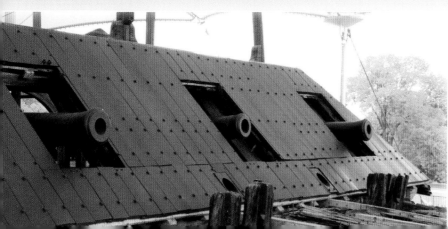

INDEX

The Author

Chris Oxlade is an experienced author of educational books for children, with more than 200 titles to his name, including many on science and technology. He enjoys camping and adventurous outdoor sports, including rock climbing, hill running, kayaking and sailing. He lives in England with his wife, children and dogs.

Picture Credits (abbreviations: t = top; b = bottom; c = centre; l = left; r = right)
© www.shutterstock.com: 4c, 8tl, 9tr, 12br, 18tl, 19c, 28tr, 28bc, 29br, 30tr, 30bl, 31bl, 31r

2, r = Cody Images. 3, c = Cody Images. 6-7, c = US Navy Photo / Alamy Stock Photo. 7, t = Niday Picture Library / Alamy Stock Photo. 8-9, c = Elena Elenaphotos21 / Alamy Stock Photo. 9, cl = Greek photonews / Alamy Stock Photo. 10, c = Bettmann / Getty Images. 12, c = National Geographic Creative / Alamy Stock Photo. 14, b = Maurice Savage / Alamy Stock Photo. 14-15, c = Glasshouse Images / Alamy Stock Photo. 16, tl = Ian Dagnall Computing / Alamy Stock Photo. 16-17, c = Archive Images / Alamy Stock Photo. 19, br = Stephen Barnes / Alamy Stock Photo. 20, c = Cody Images. 20, b = Cody Images. 21, t = Cody Images. 21, b = Cody Images. 22, c = WENN Ltd / Alamy Stock Photo. 23, t = Z2A Collection / Alamy Stock Photo. 23, b = Cody Images. 24, b = US Navy Photo / Alamy Stock Photo. 24-25, c = Stocktrek Images, Inc. /Alamy Stock Photo. 26, cl = IAP / Alamy Stock Photo. 29, c = Niday Picture Library / Alamy Stock Photo.